Southern
BISCUITS
& Quick Breads

JOSH MILLER

83
PRESS

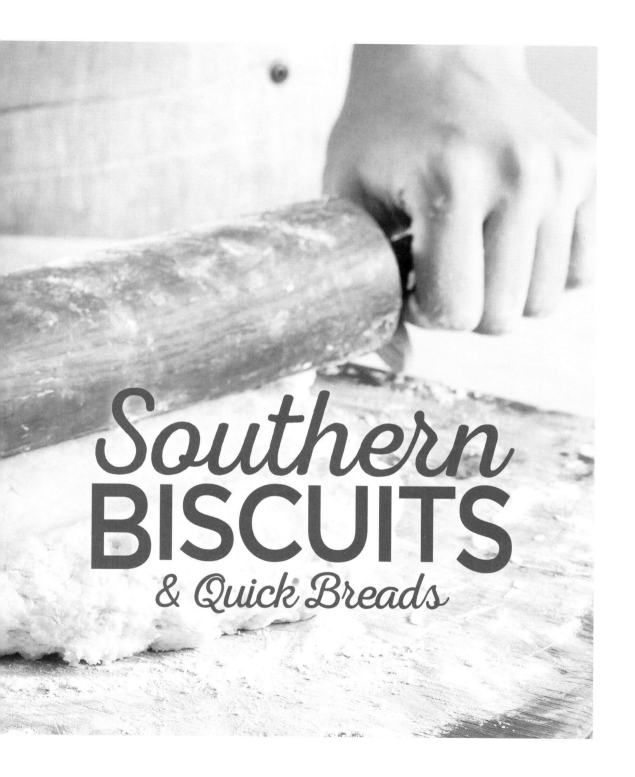

Southern
BISCUITS
& Quick Breads

83
PRESS

Copyright © 2017 by 83 Press

83 Press
1900 International Park Drive, Suite 50
Birmingham, Alabama 35243
www.hoffmanmedia.com

ISBN #978-1-940772-40-0
Printed in China

Contents

8 INTRODUCTION

16 BREAKFAST

36 LUNCH

54 SUPPER

76 DESSERT

98 QUICK BREADS

122 TOPPINGS

134 RECIPE INDEX

Introduction

The allure of biscuits begins with their aroma, beckoning us from our comfy beds on Saturday mornings. There's simply nothing better to wake up to than that buttery, toasty scent. Hot from the oven and halved to hold a pat of hastily melting butter, homemade biscuits are literally the best possible way to start any day. And thankfully, they're so easy to make.

The true beauty of biscuits is their versatility and hospitality. Whether they're slathered with butter and blackberry jam, sandwiching a crispy piece of fried chicken, or smothered with spicy sausage gravy, biscuits welcome any and all toppings, spreads, fillers, and flavors. And when it comes to stir-ins, the limits are as wide as your appetite. Bits of crispy bacon, shreds of sharp Cheddar cheese, hunks of tender sweet potato, or even melty chocolate chips—every ingredient is welcome at a biscuit party.

While they're beloved for breakfast, biscuits are perfectly at home on your plate any time of day, in every which way. For lunch, supper, or dessert, there's nothing that comes out of the kitchen that's not made better by a biscuit. So grab your buttermilk, cut up some cold butter, and flour your rolling pin—it's time to bake up some glorious biscuits!

Start with cold ingredients and work quickly so that your hands don't warm the dough

Make Your Biscuits Better

1. Stir dry ingredients together, and then cut in cold butter or shortening.

2. Add buttermilk sparingly at first; you can always add more.

3. Stir until the dough just comes together.

4. Pat or roll and fold the dough up to 3 times for flaky, layered biscuits.

5. Cut biscuits with a downward motion, and don't twist the cutter.

You can reroll biscuit scraps, but the biscuits will be slightly tougher than your first batch.

For the Love of Biscuits

Our friends share their best biscuit memories and tips

Carrie Morey

CALLIE'S HOT LITTLE BISCUIT
Charleston, South Carolina

"Some of my fondest memories are of making biscuits with my grandmother when I was a little girl. She'd let me punch my thumb in one side of the biscuit and fill the hole with maple syrup. I can't help but smile when I see my girls doing the same!"

TIP Use butter as your insurance. If your biscuits come out a little too tough or brown, slather enough butter on top and they're bound to taste good. And, as a personal preference, I use only salted butter.

John Currence

BIG BAD BREAKFAST
Oxford, Mississippi

"I tried for years as a young cook to make biscuits based on a rudimentary understanding of technique. Those biscuits were, in my mind, a consistent failure. It wasn't until I truly understood the science of why biscuits work that I started making a product that was worthy of consideration. It is a science lesson I bore all my guys with now—hoping it helps them as much as it helped me."

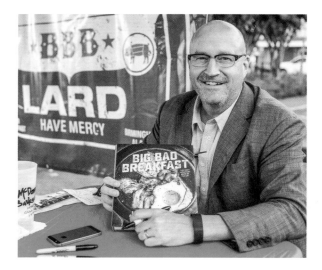

Sarah & Karl Worley
BISCUIT LOVE | *Nashville, Tennessee*

"Biscuits, like any other dish, will shine when you seek out the best ingredients—full fat buttermilk without additives, cultured butter, and winter wheat milled in small batches. Start with great ingredients, and you will be able to taste the love in the finished biscuit!"

Kevin Gillespie
REVIVAL | *Decatur, Georgia*

"We ate breakfast at my Granny's house every morning before school when we were kids, and she made biscuits almost every day. Her biscsuits were small and flat, designed to be used as a vehicle. Whether that was with sorghum syrup and butter poured over them, or maybe a slice of smoky sausage, they were built to be a part of something more. They are still my favorite, despite their flaws, because they remind me that a great biscuit is about people, places, and time more than just calories."

Christina Hagen
HOMINY GRILL | *Charleston, South Carolina*

"My favorite way to enjoy a biscuit is with a pat of cultured butter, a sprinkle of salt and some homemade jam. Trey Dutton of Southern Keep makes THE best Blueberry Vanilla Jam and his Strawberry Rhubarb is to die for!"

TIP We use a folding technique when rolling out our biscuit dough—this creates many layers and yields a perfectly risen biscuit. That technique, coupled with Southern-milled flour, a trio of fats, and fresh whole milk makes our biscuits tall and tender!

BISCUITS FOR Breakfast

RISE AND SHINE—THERE'S NO BETTER
WAY TO START YOUR DAY THAN WITH A
PLATE FULL OF HOMEMADE BISCUITS

snickerdoodle biscuits

Cinnamon toast was a staple in my house on Saturday mornings, and these biscuits take me right back there. The sweet and crunchy cinnamon-sugar topping is better than hours of uninterrupted cartoons. **MAKES 8**

2	cups all-purpose flour
1	tablespoon baking powder
1	tablespoon plus ½ teaspoon sugar, divided
¾	teaspoon kosher salt
½	cup cold unsalted butter, cubed
1	cup whole buttermilk, divided
1	tablespoon unsalted butter, melted
½	teaspoon ground cinnamon

Preheat oven to 425°.

In a large bowl, whisk together flour, baking powder, ½ teaspoon sugar, and salt. Using 2 forks or a pastry blender, cut butter into flour mixture until crumbly. Make a well in dry ingredients; add ¾ cup buttermilk, stirring until mixture just comes together. (Add remaining ¼ cup buttermilk, if necessary.)

On a lightly floured surface, gently knead dough 4 or 5 times. Roll dough ¾ inch thick. Brush dough with melted butter.

In a small bowl, combine cinnamon and remaining 1 tablespoon sugar. Sprinkle half of cinnamon mixture over dough. Fold dough in half; roll ¾ inch thick. Using a 2½-inch round cutter dipped in flour, cut 8 biscuits, without twisting cutter, rerolling scraps once. Place biscuits in a 12-inch cast-iron skillet or on a parchment-lined baking sheet. Sprinkle with remaining cinnamon mixture.

Bake until lightly browned, about 17 minutes.

sweet potato biscuits

I have a special place in my heart for sweet potato biscuits—there's something about their warm orange glow that makes me smile. Toasted pecans take them over the top. **MAKES 10 TO 12**

2	cups all-purpose flour
2	tablespoons sugar
1	tablespoon baking powder
3/4	teaspoon kosher salt
1/4	teaspoon ground ginger
1/4	teaspoon ground nutmeg
1/2	cup cold unsalted butter, cubed
1/3	cup toasted pecans, chopped
1	(15-ounce) can cut sweet potatoes in syrup,* drained well and coarsely mashed
3/4	cup whole buttermilk, divided
1	tablespoon unsalted butter, melted
Cane syrup

We used Bruce's.

Preheat oven to 425°.

In a large bowl, whisk together flour, sugar, baking powder, salt, ginger, and nutmeg. Using 2 forks or a pastry blender, cut butter into flour mixture until crumbly. Make a well in dry ingredients; add pecans, sweet potato, and 2/3 cup buttermilk, stirring until mixture just comes together. Add remaining buttermilk, if necessary. (Dough will be sticky.)

On a heavily floured surface, gently knead dough 4 or 5 times. Roll dough 3/4 inch thick. Fold dough in half; roll 3/4 inch thick. Using a 2 1/2-inch round cutter dipped in flour, cut 10 to 12 biscuits, without twisting cutter, rerolling scraps once. Place biscuits in a 12-inch cast-iron skillet or on a parchment-lined baking sheet.

Bake until lightly browned, about 17 minutes. Brush with melted butter. Drizzle with cane syrup, if desired.

chocolate chip biscuits

When my friend Kathleen first made these for me, I ate at least five of them. The whipping cream glaze and chocolate chips are the perfect decadent additions—just sweet enough. **MAKES 9**

2 **cups all-purpose flour**
1 **tablespoon baking powder**
1 **tablespoon sugar**
¾ **teaspoon kosher salt**
½ **cup cold unsalted butter, cubed**
½ **cup semisweet chocolate morsels**
1 **cup whole buttermilk, divided**
Whipping Cream Glaze (recipe follows)

WHIPPING CREAM GLAZE
1 **cup confectioners' sugar**
⅓ **cup heavy whipping cream**
¼ **teaspoon vanilla extract**
⅛ **teaspoon kosher salt**

Preheat oven to 425°.

In a large bowl, whisk together flour, baking powder, sugar, and salt. Using 2 forks or a pastry blender, cut butter into flour mixture until crumbly. Add chocolate morsels, tossing until combined. Make a well in dry ingredients; add ¾ cup buttermilk, stirring until mixture just comes together. Add remaining ¼ cup buttermilk, if necessary.

On a lightly floured surface, gently knead dough 4 or 5 times. Roll dough ¾ inch thick. Fold dough in half; roll ¾ inch thick. Using a 2½-inch round cutter dipped in flour, cut 9 biscuits, without twisting cutter, rerolling scraps once. Place biscuits in a 10-inch cast-iron skillet, touching slightly, or on a parchment-lined baking sheet.

Bake until lightly browned, about 17 minutes. Let cool in pan for 30 minutes. Drizzle with Whipping Cream Glaze.

WHIPPING CREAM GLAZE In a medium bowl, whisk together all ingredients until smooth. Use immediately.

buttermilk biscuits with sausage gravy

I'm a firm believer that everyone needs to have a good buttermilk biscuit recipe under their belt. This is baking at its most basic—trust me, if I can handle it, you definitely can! **MAKES 10**

2½ cups self-rising flour
2 tablespoons sugar
1¼ teaspoons kosher salt
¾ cup cold unsalted butter, cubed
1 cup whole buttermilk, chilled
2 tablespoons unsalted butter, melted

SAUSAGE GRAVY
1 (16-ounce) package ground pork sausage
¼ cup all-purpose flour
3 cups whole milk
½ cup heavy whipping cream
2 teaspoons apple cider vinegar
1½ teaspoons kosher salt
⅛ teaspoon garlic powder
⅛ teaspoon ground black pepper

Preheat oven to 425°. Line a rimmed baking sheet with parchment paper.

In a large bowl, whisk together flour, sugar, and salt. Using 2 forks or a pastry blender, cut butter into flour mixture until crumbly. Make a well in dry ingredients; add buttermilk, stirring until mixture just comes together.

Turn out dough onto a heavily floured surface. Shape dough into a flat log, and fold into thirds, like a letter. Roll into a 10x9-inch rectangle. Using a 3-inch round cutter dipped in flour, cut 10 biscuits, without twisting cutter; reroll scraps as necessary. Place biscuits 2 inches apart on prepared pan. Brush tops with melted butter.

Bake until golden brown, about 12 minutes.

SAUSAGE GRAVY In a large skillet, cook sausage over medium-high heat, stirring occasionally, until browned and crumbly, about 10 minutes. Sprinkle flour over sausage, stirring to coat. Gradually whisk in milk and cream. Stir in vinegar, salt, garlic powder, and pepper. Bring to a simmer, whisking constantly, until thickened, about 10 minutes. Serve immediately over warm Buttermilk Biscuits.

drop biscuits

Since I can't seem to make biscuits without getting flour pretty much everywhere, sometimes I opt for the virtually mess-free method that drop biscuits provide. They're a great alternative to rolled biscuits. **MAKES 18**

2 cups all-purpose flour
1 tablespoon baking powder
1 teaspoon kosher salt
¼ cup cold unsalted butter, cubed
¾ cup whole milk

Preheat oven to 450°. In a large bowl, whisk together flour, baking powder, and salt. Using 2 forks or a pastry blender, cut butter into flour mixture until crumbly. Make a well in dry ingredients; add milk, stirring until mixture just comes together.

Using a ¼ cup measure, drop dough 2 inches apart on an ungreased baking sheet. Bake until golden brown, about 10 minutes.

rolled biscuits **MAKES 12**

2½ cups all-purpose flour
1 tablespoon baking powder
1 teaspoon kosher salt
6 tablespoons cold unsalted butter, cubed
1 cup whole milk

Preheat oven to 450°. In a large bowl, whisk together flour, baking powder, and salt. Using 2 forks or a pastry blender, cut butter into flour mixture until crumbly. Make a well in dry ingredients; add milk, stirring until mixture just comes together.

Turn out dough onto a lightly floured surface, and knead lightly for about 10 turns. Roll dough ½ inch thick. Using a 2½-inch round cutter, cut 12 biscuits, without twisting cutter, rerolling scraps as necessary. Place biscuits 2 inches apart on an ungreased baking sheet. Bake until golden brown, about 12 minutes.

DROP BISCUIT ADD-INS

///

Add extra flavor to these easy-to-make biscuits by stirring in ½ to 1 cup shredded cheese; ½ cup chopped nuts or dried fruit, or 2 to 3 tablespoons chopped fresh herbs, such as thyme or basil, with the milk. Stir until combined.

DROP BISCUITS

ROLLED BISCUITS

toad in a biscuit

Growing up, I never had toad in a hole (a British dish consisting of an egg fried inside a piece of toast), but my Dad made us cat head biscuits all the time. Using jumbo (cat head-sized) biscuits is a fun way to put a Southern twist on the British classic.

CAT HEAD BISCUITS
Makes 8 biscuits

2	cups all-purpose flour
1	tablespoon baking powder
1	teaspoon kosher salt
½	teaspoon baking soda
¼	cup cold unsalted butter, cubed
1¼	cups whole buttermilk

TOAD IN A BISCUIT
Serves 1

1	Cat Head Biscuit (recipe precedes)
1	tablespoon unsalted butter
1	large egg, separated
	Kosher salt
	Ground black pepper

Preheat oven to 425°.

In a large bowl, whisk together flour, baking powder, salt, and baking soda. Using 2 forks or a pastry blender, cut butter into flour mixture until crumbly. Make a well in dry ingredients; add buttermilk, stirring until mixture just comes together.

Using a ½ cup measure, drop dough 2 inches apart on an ungreased baking sheet.

Bake until golden brown, about 15 minutes.

TOAD IN A BISCUIT Using a 2-inch round cutter, cut a hole in center of biscuit. Reserve cutout for another use.

In a small nonstick skillet, melt butter over medium heat. Place biscuit in skillet, top side down; cook for 1 to 2 minutes. Turn biscuit over. Pour egg white into hole in biscuit. Cook, without touching, for about 1 minute. Add yolk to white. Cover and cook to desired degree of doneness, 6 to 7 minutes. Season to taste with salt and pepper. Serve immediately.

angel biscuits

The first angel biscuits I ever tasted were baked by "Mr. Phil," who made his signature biscuits once a month at my church. At the time, I didn't know what made them so darn good, but I couldn't eat enough of them. Turns out, it was yeast that made them extra fluffy and tasty. **MAKES 24**

1   **(0.25-ounce) package active dry yeast**
½   **cup warm water (105° to 110°)**
5½ **cups all-purpose flour**
¼   **cup sugar**
2   **teaspoons kosher salt**
1   **teaspoon baking powder**
1   **teaspoon baking soda**
½   **cup all-vegetable shortening**
2   **cups whole buttermilk**

In a small bowl, stir together yeast and ½ cup warm water. Let stand until mixture is foamy, about 5 minutes.

In a large bowl, whisk together flour, sugar, salt, baking powder, and baking soda. Using 2 forks or a pastry blender, cut shortening into flour mixture until crumbly. Make a well in dry ingredients; add yeast mixture and buttermilk, stirring until mixture just comes together. Cover and refrigerate for 30 minutes.

Preheat oven to 450°. Line a baking sheet with parchment paper.

Turn out dough onto a heavily floured surface, and knead lightly for about 10 turns. Roll dough ½ inch thick. Using a 2½-inch round cutter dipped in flour, cut 24 biscuits, without twisting cutter, rerolling scraps as necessary. Place biscuits 2 inches apart on prepared pan.

Bake until golden brown, about 12 minutes.

**CAT HEAD
BISCUIT**
(page 29)

**ANGEL
BISCUITS**

whole wheat biscuits

Whole wheat flour gets a bad rap for making baked goods chewy. Our test kitchen solved the problem with a simple solution—add in some regular all-purpose flour. The result is a wholesome biscuit with a great tender texture. **MAKES 12**

1   cup all-purpose flour
1   cup whole wheat flour
5   teaspoons baking powder
1   tablespoon sugar
¾   teaspoon kosher salt
½   cup unsalted butter, cubed
1   cup plus 3 tablespoons whole buttermilk, divided

Preheat oven to 450°.

In a large bowl, whisk together flours, baking powder, sugar, and salt. Using 2 forks or a pastry blender, cut butter into flour mixture until crumbly. Make a well in dry ingredients; add 1 cup buttermilk, stirring until mixture just comes together. (Add remaining 3 tablespoons buttermilk, if needed.)

Turn out dough onto a lightly floured surface, and knead 2 to 3 times. Roll dough into an 8-inch circle. Using a 2-inch round cutter dipped in flour, cut 12 biscuits, without twisting cutter, rerolling scraps as necessary. Place biscuits 1 inch apart on an ungreased baking sheet.

Bake until golden brown, about 12 minutes. Let cool for 10 minutes before serving.

bacon-cheddar biscuits

When my friend Anna suggested adding bacon fat to our classic biscuit recipe, there was only one thing to say—yes! Bacon makes everything better, right? **MAKES 14**

2½ cups self-rising flour
1 tablespoon sugar
1 teaspoon ground black pepper
½ cup cold bacon drippings
2 tablespoons cold unsalted butter, cubed
1 cup shredded sharp Cheddar cheese
½ cup crumbled cooked bacon
¾ cup cold whole buttermilk
2 tablespoons unsalted butter, melted

Preheat oven to 425°. Line a baking sheet with parchment paper.

In a large bowl, stir together flour, sugar, and pepper. Using a pastry blender or 2 forks, cut in bacon drippings and cold butter until crumbly. Stir in cheese, cooked bacon, and buttermilk just until combined.

Turn out dough onto a heavily floured surface. Fold dough in half until it just comes together, 3 to 4 times. Pat or roll dough into a 1-inch thick rectangle. Using a knife dipped in flour, cut dough into 2-inch rectangles.

Place biscuits 2 inches apart on prepared pan. Freeze until cold, about 10 minutes. Brush with melted butter. Bake until golden brown, about 12 minutes.

BISCUITS
FOR
Lunch

FROM GRAB-AND-GO SANDWICHES TO
POT PIES AND MORE, BISCUITS MAKE
YOUR MID-DAY MEAL MORE MARVELOUS

chicken biscuits

Fried chicken and flaky biscuits are a Southern match made in heaven. Hot sauce and buttermilk give these tenders a nice tangy flavor—add a dash of cayenne pepper if you dare. **SERVES 6**

2   boneless skinless chicken breasts
1   cup whole buttermilk
1   tablespoon hot sauce
5   teaspoons kosher salt, divided
1½ cups all-purpose flour
2   teaspoons ground black pepper
Canola oil, for frying
6   Buttermilk Biscuits (recipe on page 25)

Place a wire rack on a rimmed baking sheet.

Place chicken on a cutting board; cover with plastic wrap. Using a rolling pin, gently pound chicken to flatten to ¼ inch thick. Cut into 6 portions.

In a large resealable plastic bag, combine chicken, buttermilk, hot sauce, and 2 teaspoons salt. Refrigerate for 30 minutes.

In a shallow dish, stir together flour, pepper, and remaining 3 teaspoons salt. Remove chicken from buttermilk mixture, draining excess. Dredge chicken in flour mixture, shaking off excess.

In a large cast-iron skillet, pour oil to halfway full, and heat over medium-high heat until a deep-fry thermometer registers 350°. Working in batches, fry chicken, turning occasionally, until golden brown on all sides and a meat thermometer inserted in thickest portion registers 165°, about 10 minutes. Let cool slightly on prepared rack.

Serve warm between halved Buttermilk Biscuits.

black pepper & parmesan biscuits with roast beef

Roast beef and horseradish make such a great pairing.
P.S. These sandwiches make a great party appetizer. **MAKES 10**

3   **cups self-rising flour**
½   **cup cold unsalted butter, cubed**
½   **cup shredded Parmesan cheese**
2   **teaspoons coarsely ground black pepper**
1¼   **cups whole buttermilk**
1   **cup mayonnaise**
2   **tablespoons horseradish**
1   **pound thinly sliced deli roast beef**

Preheat oven to 450°. Line a baking sheet with parchment paper.

In a medium bowl, place flour. Using 2 forks or a pastry blender, cut butter into flour until crumbly. Stir in cheese and pepper. Make a well in dry ingredients; add buttermilk, stirring until mixture just comes together.

On a lightly floured surface, pat dough into a ¾-inch-thick circle. Using a 2½-inch round cutter dipped in flour, cut 10 biscuits, without twisting cutter, discarding scraps. Place biscuits on prepared pan.

Bake until lightly browned, 12 to 15 minutes.

In a small bowl, combine mayonnaise and horseradish. Cut biscuits in half, and spread cut sides of biscuits with mayonnaise mixture. Top bottom halves with roast beef, and cover with top halves of biscuits.

biscuit-topped chicken pot pies

Some folks scoff at drop biscuits as a lazy man's biscuit, but I beg to differ. Their easy preparation makes them perfect for topping pot pies, like these little guys. A sprinkle of sharp white Cheddar makes them even better. **MAKES 8**

2	tablespoons vegetable oil
2	cups chopped yellow onion
2/3	cup chopped carrot
1/3	cup finely chopped celery
2½	cups all-purpose flour, divided
3	cups low-sodium chicken broth
½	cup heavy whipping cream
½	cup whole milk
4	cups shredded cooked chicken
4	cups chopped fresh kale
2	teaspoons kosher salt, divided
1	teaspoon ground black pepper
1½	cups finely shredded sharp white Cheddar cheese, divided
1½	teaspoons baking powder
½	teaspoon baking soda
5	tablespoons cold unsalted butter, cubed
1	cup whole buttermilk

Preheat oven to 400°. Line a baking sheet with parchment paper. In a large Dutch oven, heat oil over medium-high heat. Add onion, carrot, and celery; cook, stirring frequently, until vegetables soften, about 5 minutes. Add ½ cup flour; cook for 1 minute. Add broth, and bring to a boil, stirring until mixture thickens, about 1 minute. Reduce heat to medium-low; stir in cream and milk. Add chicken and kale; cook for 8 minutes, stirring frequently. Add 1 teaspoon salt and pepper, stirring to combine. Divide mixture among 8 (1-cup) oven-proof ramekins.

In a large bowl, whisk together 1 cup cheese, baking powder, baking soda, remaining 2 cups flour, and remaining 1 teaspoon salt. Using 2 forks or a pastry blender, cut butter into flour mixture until crumbly. Make a well in dry ingredients; add buttermilk, stirring until mixture just comes together. (Dough will be sticky.) Drop heaping ¼ cupfuls of dough onto prepared pan.

Bake until edges are lightly browned, about 8 minutes. Place biscuits on top of ramekins, and sprinkle with remaining ½ cup cheese. Place ramekins on a rimmed baking sheet. Bake until browned and bubbly, 12 to 16 minutes, covering with foil to prevent excess browning, if necessary.

spicy cheddar biscuits with glazed ham

For lunch, for brunch, or even for parties, it's hard to pass up a good ham biscuit. This sweet and smoky ham is especially delicious on these cheesy biscuits. **MAKES 10**

2   cups all-purpose flour
1   tablespoon baking powder
½   teaspoon kosher salt
½   teaspoon ground red pepper
½   cup cold unsalted butter, cubed
⅔   cup shredded sharp Cheddar cheese
1   cup whole buttermilk
Melted butter
Sliced ham and honey, to serve

GLAZED HAM
Makes 10 to 12 servings

1¼   cups water, divided
1   (10- to 11-pound) bone-in smoked ham (shank portion)
⅔   cup firmly packed light brown sugar
⅔   cup cane syrup
⅓   cup distilled white vinegar
2   teaspoons smoked paprika
¼   teaspoon kosher salt

Preheat oven to 425°. Line a large baking sheet with parchment paper. In the work bowl of a food processor, place flour, baking powder, salt, and red pepper; pulse until combined. Add butter; pulse until crumbly, 4 to 5 times. Add cheese and ¾ cup buttermilk; pulse just until dry ingredients are moistened. Gradually add remaining ¼ cup buttermilk, if needed.

Turn out dough onto a lightly floured surface, and gently knead 3 times. Roll dough ½ inch thick. Fold dough in half. Using a 2½-inch round cutter dipped in flour, cut 10 biscuits, without twisting cutter, rerolling scraps once. Place biscuits 1 inch apart on prepared pan. Bake until lightly browned, about 12 minutes. Brush with melted butter. Cut biscuits in half. Serve with ham and honey, if desired.

GLAZED HAM Preheat oven to 325°. Line a roasting pan with foil, and spray with cooking spray. Pour 1 cup water in pan. Using a sharp knife, lightly score outside of ham. Place ham in prepared pan, and loosely cover with foil. Bake for 1 hour.

In a bowl, whisk together brown sugar, cane syrup, vinegar, paprika, salt, and remaining ¼ cup water. Brush ham with sugar mixture. Bake, loosely covered with foil, until a meat thermometer registers 160°, about 1½ hours more, brushing with sugar mixture occasionally. (Add additional water to pan, if needed.) Serve with Spicy Cheddar Biscuits.

pimiento cheese & bacon biscuit sandwiches

Bacon, pimiento cheese, and biscuits—oh my! No self-respecting Southerner will be able to pass these puppies up. **MAKES 14**

4   cups all-purpose flour
1½ teaspoons baking powder
1   teaspoon baking soda
1   tablespoon kosher salt
1½ cups cold unsalted
       butter, cubed
1½ to 2 cups whole buttermilk
1   large egg, beaten
14   slices applewood-
       smoked bacon
¼   cup pure maple syrup
Pecan Pimiento Cheese
       (recipe follows)

PECAN PIMIENTO CHEESE
Makes about 3 cups

½   cup mayonnaise
2   ounces cream cheese,
       softened
1   (4-ounce) jar diced
       pimientos, drained
½   teaspoon ground
       red pepper
1   (8-ounce) block
       sharp Cheddar cheese,
       shredded
¼   cup toasted chopped
       pecans

Preheat oven to 375°. Line a large rimmed baking sheet with parchment paper. Line another large rimmed baking sheet with foil.

In the bowl of a stand mixer fitted with the paddle attachment, beat flour, baking powder, baking soda, and salt at low speed until combined. Add butter, and beat until mixture is crumbly. Gradually add buttermilk just until dough comes together.

Turn out dough onto a lightly floured surface, and pat 1 inch thick. Using a 3-inch round cutter dipped in flour, cut 14 biscuits, rerolling scraps as necessary. Place biscuits on parchment-lined pan. Brush dough with beaten egg. Bake until golden brown, 25 to 30 minutes. Let cool completely.

Arrange bacon slices on foil-lined pan, and brush with maple syrup. Bake until golden brown and crisp, 20 to 25 minutes.

Cut biscuits and bacon slices in half; spread biscuits with Pecan Pimiento Cheese, and top with 2 pieces bacon. Serve immediately.

PECAN PIMIENTO CHEESE In a medium bowl, stir together mayonnaise, cream cheese, pimientos, and red pepper. Fold in Cheddar and pecans until well combined. Cover and refrigerate for up to 5 days.

tomato cobbler

Although tomatoes taste best in season, these days you can find some pretty tasty hothouse cherry and grape tomatoes any time of year. I love the way they burst during baking, releasing their sweet juices that get sopped up by this savory biscuit topping. **SERVES 6 TO 8**

BISCUIT TOPPING
1⅔ **cups self-rising flour**
⅔ **cup plain yellow cornmeal**
4 **slices bacon, cooked and crumbled**
½ **teaspoon kosher salt**
¾ **cup whole buttermilk**
⅓ **cup unsalted butter, melted**

FILLING
1 **tablespoon olive oil**
3 **pounds assorted grape and cherry tomatoes**
¼ **cup unsalted butter**
1 **cup thinly sliced red onion**
2 **cloves garlic, minced**
2 **tablespoons all-purpose flour**
2 **tablespoons balsamic vinegar**
2 **teaspoons kosher salt**

BISCUIT TOPPING In a medium bowl, whisk together flour, cornmeal, bacon, and salt. Add buttermilk and melted butter, stirring until a soft dough forms. Set aside.

FILLING Preheat oven to 400°. Heat an enamel-coated 10-inch cast-iron skillet over medium heat. Add oil and tomatoes; cook, stirring constantly, until tomatoes begin to soften, 5 to 7 minutes. Remove from skillet; set aside.

Melt butter in skillet. Add red onion; cook until tender, about 5 minutes. Add garlic; cook until fragrant, about 1 minute. Stir in flour; cook for 1 minute. Add vinegar, salt, and cooked tomatoes, stirring to combine; cook 5 minutes more. Remove from heat, and spoon Biscuit Topping over tomato mixture.

Bake until topping is golden brown, 25 to 30 minutes.

brisket & biscuits

I'll be honest with you—I came up with this idea on a whim; I love a good culinary rhyme. But when we tasted the classic Texas brisket accompaniments (good Cheddar and tart pickles) on a biscuit, we knew we had a hit on our plates. **SERVES 6**

Mesquite wood chips,
    soaked in water
    for 30 minutes
1 (12-pound) whole
    beef brisket
¼ cup kosher salt
¼ cup ground black
    pepper

BISCUITS
Makes 6

⅔ cups all-purpose
    flour
⅓ cup plain cornmeal
1 tablespoon baking
    powder
½ teaspoon kosher
    salt
½ cup cold unsalted
    butter, cubed
1 cup whole
    buttermilk
1 pound sliced
    smoked brisket
6 slices Cheddar
    cheese
Dill pickle slices

Preheat smoker to 225° to 250°. Sprinkle soaked wood chips over coals. Trim fat on brisket to ¼ inch thick. In a disposable roasting pan, place brisket, fat side up. In a small bowl, combine salt and pepper. Rub all sides of brisket with mixture. Let stand at room temperature for 30 minutes.

Cook brisket, covered, for 5 hours. Remove brisket from pan; discard pan. Wrap brisket in heavy-duty foil. Return brisket to smoker; cook, covered, until very tender, 8 to 10 hours more. Let stand for 30 minutes before slicing.

BISCUITS Preheat oven to 425°. Line a baking sheet with parchment paper. In a large bowl, whisk together flour, cornmeal, baking powder, and salt. Using 2 forks or a pastry blender, cut butter into flour mixture until crumbly. Make a well in dry ingredients; add buttermilk, stirring until mixture just comes together.

Turn out dough onto a lightly floured surface, and knead gently 4 or 5 times. Roll dough ¾ inch thick. Using a 3-inch round cutter dipped in flour, cut 6 biscuits, without twisting cutter, rerolling scraps as necessary. Place biscuits 1 inch apart on prepared pan.

Bake until golden brown, about 12 minutes. Let stand for 10 minutes. Cut biscuits in half horizontally. Divide brisket and cheese among bottom halves of biscuits. Bake until cheese is melted, about 2 minutes. Top with pickles, and cover with biscuit tops.

cheese-pepper biscuits

Everybody expects a round biscuit, so I think it's fun to switch things up every now and then. These square biscuits don't require a special cutter—any good knife will do the trick. **MAKES 25**

2 **cups all-purpose flour**
1 **tablespoon baking powder**
¾ **teaspoon kosher salt**
½ **teaspoon sugar**
¼ **teaspoon cracked black pepper**
¼ **teaspoon ground red pepper**
½ **cup cold unsalted butter, cubed**
⅔ **cup shredded sharp Cheddar cheese**
¼ **cup freshly grated Parmesan cheese**
1 **cup whole buttermilk**
1 **tablespoon unsalted butter, melted**
Stone-ground mustard and ham, to serve

Preheat oven to 425°.

In a large bowl, whisk together flour, baking powder, salt, sugar, black pepper, and red pepper. Using 2 forks or a pastry blender, cut butter into flour mixture until crumbly. Make a well in dry ingredients; add cheeses and ¾ cup buttermilk, stirring until mixture just comes together. Add remaining ¼ cup buttermilk, if needed.

On a lightly floured surface, gently knead dough 4 or 5 times. Roll or pat dough into an 8-inch square; cut into 25 squares. Place close together in a 10-inch square cast-iron skillet or a parchment-lined baking sheet.

Bake until golden brown, about 17 minutes. Let cool for 15 minutes. Using a large spatula, remove from pan, and cut into pieces. Split biscuits horizontally, and brush with melted butter. Serve with mustard and ham, if desired.

BISCUITS
FOR
Supper

ATOP A CASSEROLE OR ACCOMPANYING
YOUR FAVORITE MAIN DISH, BISCUITS ARE
RIGHT AT HOME ON YOUR SUPPER PLATE

black pepper & thyme biscuits

I get asked a lot, "Do you have to make biscuits in a cast-iron skillet?" The short answer is no. But try it—the bottoms get extra crispy, kinda like a cracker, and if you pack them in, the sides of the skillet help out with rising. **MAKES 15**

2	cups all-purpose flour
¼	cup roughly chopped fresh thyme
4	teaspoons baking powder
1	teaspoon kosher salt
¾	teaspoon ground black pepper, divided
¼	teaspoon baking soda
¼	teaspoon garlic powder
¼	teaspoon onion powder
½	cup cold unsalted butter, cubed
1¼	cups whole buttermilk

Preheat oven to 450°. Lightly spray a square cast-iron skillet with cooking spray.

In a large bowl, whisk together flour, thyme, baking powder, salt, ½ teaspoon pepper, baking soda, garlic powder, and onion powder. Using 2 forks or a pastry blender, cut butter into flour mixture until crumbly. Make a well in dry ingredients; add buttermilk, stirring until mixture just comes together.

Turn out dough onto a lightly floured surface, and gently pat ¾ inch thick. Using a 2½-inch round cutter dipped in flour, cut 15 biscuits without twisting cutter, rerolling scraps as necessary. Arrange biscuits in prepared skillet. Sprinkle with remaining ¼ teaspoon pepper.

Bake until golden brown, 18 to 20 minutes.

chicken & dumplings skillet casserole

To this day, my grandmother's chicken and dumplings live on in my memory as one of my most-adored comfort foods. Here we trade her pillowy simmered dumplings for a quick-biscuit topping that bakes up nice and flaky. **SERVES 4**

4 boneless skinless chicken thighs, halved
1 teaspoon kosher salt, divided
½ teaspoon ground black pepper, divided
5 teaspoons vegetable oil, divided
1½ cups fresh green beans, chopped
1 cup chopped parsnip
1 cup quartered mushrooms
½ cup chopped carrot
1¼ cups chicken broth
¼ cup all-purpose flour
½ cup whole milk
1 tablespoon chopped fresh parsley
1 teaspoon chopped fresh rosemary

BISCUIT TOPPING
1 cup self-rising flour
¼ cup cold unsalted butter, cubed
4 tablespoons whole milk
1 tablespoon butter, melted

Preheat oven to 400°. Sprinkle chicken with ¼ teaspoon salt and ¼ teaspoon pepper. In a 10-inch skillet, heat 2 teaspoons oil over medium-high heat. Add chicken; cook until browned, about 2 minutes per side. Remove from pan; set aside.

Wipe pan clean. Heat remaining 3 teaspoons oil over medium-high heat. Add green beans, parsnip, mushrooms, and carrot; cook, stirring occasionally, until vegetables begin to soften, about 4 minutes. Add broth. Reduce heat to medium-low; cover and simmer until tender, about 10 minutes. In a medium bowl, stir together flour, remaining ¾ teaspoon salt, and remaining ¼ teaspoon pepper. Whisk in milk, parsley, and rosemary. Add to broth mixture in pan, stirring until mixture begins to thicken. Return chicken to pan. Cover and remove from heat.

BISCUIT TOPPING In the work bowl of a food processor, pulse flour and butter until mixture is crumbly. Add milk, 1 tablespoon at a time, pulsing until a soft dough forms. Turn out dough onto a lightly floured surface, and knead 3 or 4 times. Roll ½ inch thick, and cut into 1-inch pieces. Place dough pieces on top of hot filling. Bake until biscuits are lightly browned and chicken is cooked through, about 15 minutes. Brush tops of biscuits with melted butter before serving.

white cheddar biscuits with fresh herbs

Second to their inherent goodness, one of the best things about biscuits is that you can make them ahead of time, and they freeze beautifully. Whip up a batch of these herbed beauties and keep them in the freezer for your next dinner party. **MAKES 12**

3   **cups all-purpose flour**
1   **tablespoon baking powder**
1   **teaspoon kosher salt**
½   **teaspoon baking soda**
½   **cup cold unsalted butter, cubed**
½   **cup shredded sharp white Cheddar cheese**
1   **tablespoon chopped fresh parsley**
1   **tablespoon chopped fresh chives**
1   **tablespoon chopped fresh rosemary**
1½   **cups plus 2 to 4 tablespoons heavy whipping cream, divided**

Preheat oven to 450°. Line a baking sheet with parchment paper.

In a large bowl, whisk together flour, baking powder, salt, and baking soda. Using 2 forks or a pastry blender, cut butter into flour mixture until crumbly. Fold in cheese, parsley, chives, and rosemary. Make a well in dry ingredients; add 1½ cups cream, stirring until mixture just comes together. Add additional 2 tablespoons cream, if necessary.

Turn out dough onto a lightly floured surface, and knead lightly 3 to 4 turns. Pat dough ½ inch thick. Using a 3-inch round cutter dipped in flour, cut 12 biscuits, without twisting cutter, rerolling scraps once.

Place biscuits 1 inch apart on prepared pan. Using a pastry brush, lightly brush tops of biscuits with remaining 2 tablespoons cream.

Bake until light golden brown, 12 to 15 minutes. Serve warm.

sunday chicken & biscuit pot pie

Some Sundays call for big productions like fried chicken or pot roast. Other times, you just need something simple. This one-skillet wonder fits the bill, packed with plenty of chicken and veggies and topped with flaky biscuits. **SERVES 6**

BISCUIT TOPPING
1⅓ cups self-rising flour
6 tablespoons cold unsalted butter
½ cup whole milk

FILLING
¼ cup unsalted butter
1 cup chopped onion
1 cup thinly sliced carrot
½ cup chopped celery
¼ cup all-purpose flour
1 cup chicken broth
1 cup half-and-half
3 cups chopped cooked chicken
1 (9-ounce) package frozen sugar snap peas, thawed
½ teaspoon ground black pepper
½ teaspoon dried thyme

BISCUIT TOPPING Preheat oven to 450°. Line a baking sheet with parchment paper. In a large bowl, place flour. Using 2 forks or a pastry blender, cut butter into flour mixture until crumbly. Make a well in dry ingredients; add milk, stirring until mixture just comes together.

Turn out dough onto a lightly floured surface, and pat ½ inch thick. Cut into rounds with a biscuit cutter, or cut into squares with a knife or pizza cutter. Place biscuits on prepared pan. Bake for 6 to 8 minutes.

FILLING In a 10-inch cast-iron skillet, melt butter over medium heat. Add onion, carrot, and celery; cook until tender, about 8 minutes. Gradually add flour, stirring until combined. Cook for 1 minute, stirring constantly. Gradually add broth and half-and-half; cook, stirring constantly, until mixture thickens, about 5 minutes.

Add chicken, peas, pepper, and thyme, stirring to combine. Cook, stirring occasionally, until heated through, about 3 minutes. Place partially baked biscuits on top of chicken mixture. Bake until biscuits are golden brown, 12 to 15 minutes.

cornmeal drop biscuits

Soup lovers, take note—these are the biscuits for you! The perfect marriage of cornbread and biscuits, they're great for crumbling into your favorite hearty stews and soups. **MAKES 12**

2   cups self-rising flour
½   cup stone-ground
      white cornmeal
⅔   cup cold unsalted
      butter, cubed
1 to 1¼ cups whole
      buttermilk

Preheat oven to 400°. Line a baking sheet with parchment paper.

In a large bowl, whisk together flour and cornmeal. Using 2 forks or a pastry blender, cut butter into flour mixture until crumbly. Make a well in dry ingredients; add 1 cup buttermilk, stirring until mixture just comes together. (Add remaining ¼ cup buttermilk, if needed.)

Drop dough by 3 tablespoonfuls 1 inch apart on prepared pan.

Bake until golden brown, 12 to 14 minutes.

sweet potato drop biscuits

It's always a tough decision when I make sweet potato biscuits—do I take them in a sweet or savory direction? These easy peppery drop biscuits are a savory win—they're great with ham at Easter or with turkey at Thanksgiving. And on their own, of course! **MAKES 10**

1½   **cups self-rising flour**
¾   **cup cooked mashed sweet potato**
6   **tablespoons whole buttermilk**
6   **tablespoons unsalted butter, melted and divided**
¼   **teaspoon ground black pepper**

Preheat oven to 425°. Line a baking sheet with parchment paper.

Place flour in a medium bowl. In a small bowl, whisk together sweet potato, buttermilk, and 4 tablespoons melted butter. Make a well in flour; add sweet potato mixture, stirring until mixture just comes together. Drop biscuits by 3 tablespoonfuls 1 inch apart onto prepared pan.

Bake until lightly browned, about 10 minutes. Brush with remaining 2 tablespoons melted butter, and sprinkle with pepper. Bake until golden brown, about 5 minutes more. Let cool on a wire rack for 10 minutes.

turkey pot pie

At my house, leftover biscuits are a rarity; we tend to keep going back for "just one more" until there's none left. If you do find yourself with a handful of leftover biscuits, this recipe is perfect; biscuits make the best topping ever! SERVES 6

¼ cup unsalted butter
1 cup chopped onion
1 tablespoon minced fresh garlic
⅓ cup all-purpose flour
3 cups chicken broth
1 cup whole milk
1½ cups chopped Yukon gold potatoes
1 cup sliced carrot
1 cup sliced celery
3 cups chopped cooked turkey
1 cup frozen pearl onions
1 cup frozen petite green peas
1 tablespoon chopped fresh thyme
1 tablespoon chopped fresh sage
1¾ teaspoons kosher salt
¼ teaspoon ground black pepper
6 leftover biscuits, quartered

Preheat oven to 350°.

In a large Dutch oven, melt butter over medium heat. Add chopped onion and garlic; cook, stirring frequently, until softened, 4 to 5 minutes.

Add flour; cook for 1 minute, stirring constantly. Add broth and milk, whisking until smooth.

Cook, stirring frequently, until mixture begins to thicken, about 5 minutes. Add potatoes, carrot, and celery; reduce heat to medium-low.

Cook, stirring occasionally, until vegetables are tender, about 20 minutes.

Stir in turkey, pearl onions, peas, thyme, sage, salt, and pepper. Remove from heat. Spoon mixture into an 11x8-inch baking dish. Top with biscuit pieces.

Bake until lightly browned and bubbly, about 30 minutes.

savory cobbler with sausage & white beans

You'll love what's waiting for you underneath these buttery-crumbly cornbread biscuits—a simmering skillet full of smoked sausage, tender vegetables, and creamy white beans. It's a comfort food masterpiece. **SERVES 6**

4	cups sliced smoked sausage
1	medium onion, halved and thinly sliced
1	green bell pepper, thinly sliced
1	red bell pepper, thinly sliced
1	tablespoon minced fresh garlic
1	teaspoon dried oregano
¼	teaspoon crushed red pepper
1	(14.5-ounce) can diced tomatoes
1	(16-ounce) can white beans, drained and rinsed
½	cup water
1	teaspoon kosher salt
¼	teaspoon ground black pepper

BISCUIT TOPPING

1	cup stone-ground white or yellow cornmeal
1	cup all-purpose flour
2	teaspoons baking powder
1	teaspoon kosher salt
½	teaspoon baking soda
1½	cups whole buttermilk
¼	cup unsalted butter, melted
1	large egg
1	cup grated Parmesan cheese

Preheat oven to 425°. In a 12-inch cast-iron skillet, cook sausage over medium-high heat until browned, about 4 minutes. Remove sausage using a slotted spoon, and let drain on paper towels.

Add onion, bell peppers, garlic, oregano, and red pepper to skillet. Cook, stirring occasionally, until vegetables are tender, about 5 minutes. Add tomatoes to skillet; cook for 2 minutes. Stir in sausage, beans, ½ cup water, salt, and pepper; bring to a boil. Remove from heat.

BISCUIT TOPPING In a medium bowl, stir together cornmeal, flour, baking powder, salt, and baking soda. In another medium bowl, stir together buttermilk, melted butter, and egg. Gradually add buttermilk mixture to cornmeal mixture, stirring just until combined. Stir in cheese. Drop batter by heaping tablespoonfuls over sausage mixture.

Bake until topping is golden brown, 15 to 18 minutes.

dill & cornmeal drop biscuits

Don't tell biscuits, but my love for cornbread runs a close second; anytime I can find a way to sneak cornmeal into a recipe, I do it. The dill in these biscuits gives them a fresh spring flavor; they'd be equally tasty with fresh chopped thyme, sage, or rosemary. **MAKES 10**

1½ cups all-purpose flour
½ cup plain yellow cornmeal
1 tablespoon finely chopped fresh dill
1 tablespoon baking powder
¾ teaspoon kosher salt
½ teaspoon baking soda
½ teaspoon sugar
¾ cup whole buttermilk
⅓ cup plus 1 tablespoon unsalted butter, melted and divided

Preheat oven to 425°.

In a large bowl, whisk together flour, cornmeal, dill, baking powder, salt, baking soda, and sugar.

In a small bowl, combine buttermilk and ⅓ cup melted butter. Make a well in dry ingredients; add buttermilk mixture, stirring until mixture just comes together. Spoon dough by heaping ⅓ cupfuls about 1 inch apart in a 12-inch cast-iron skillet or on a parchment-lined baking sheet.

Bake until lightly browned, about 17 minutes. Let cool slightly. Brush with remaining 1 tablespoon melted butter.

pecan & goat cheese biscuits

These little guys are one of my favorite dinner biscuits. The tangy goat cheese and woodsy thyme flavors meld so beautifully, and the pecans add a perfect, hearty crunch. I love to serve them with roasted pork tenderloin. **MAKES 16**

4   **cups self-rising flour**
1   **teaspoon kosher salt**
3/4   **cup cold unsalted butter, cubed**
1½   **cups pecans, chopped**
6   **ounces crumbled goat cheese, chilled**
2   **teaspoons chopped fresh thyme**
1¾   **cups whole buttermilk**
2   **tablespoons unsalted butter, melted**
Cane syrup

Preheat oven to 425°. Spray a 12-inch cast-iron skillet with cooking spray.

In a large bowl, whisk together flour and salt. Using 2 forks or a pastry blender, cut butter into flour mixture until crumbly. Stir in pecans, goat cheese, and thyme. Make a well in dry ingredients; add buttermilk, stirring until mixture just comes together. Using a 4-tablespoon scoop, drop into prepared skillet. Brush with melted butter.

Bake until tops are golden, 30 to 35 minutes, loosely covering with foil to prevent excess browning, if necessary. Drizzle with cane syrup, if desired.

BISCUITS FOR *Dessert*

FROM COBBLERS TO SHORTCAKES,
DESSERT'S EVEN BETTER WITH
A LITTLE HELP FROM A BISCUIT

triple berry cobbler

Like most folks, I grew up with my mother making "flag cakes" for summer holidays like Memorial Day and the Fourth of July. This cobbler meets the need for a patriotic-themed dessert without all the fuss. **SERVES 6 TO 8**

3	cups fresh strawberries, quartered
3	cups fresh raspberries
3	cups fresh blueberries
1	cup plus 2 tablespoons granulated sugar, divided
¼	cup cornstarch
2	tablespoons fresh lemon juice
1	cup all-purpose flour
1½	teaspoons baking powder
¼	teaspoon kosher salt
3	tablespoons cold unsalted butter, cubed
⅔	cup whole milk
2	tablespoons coarse sugar

Preheat oven to 375°.

In a large bowl, combine strawberries, raspberries, blueberries, 1 cup granulated sugar, cornstarch, and lemon juice. Spoon berry mixture into a 1½-quart baking dish.

In a medium bowl, whisk together flour, baking powder, salt, and remaining 2 tablespoons granulated sugar. Using 2 forks or a pastry blender, cut butter into flour mixture until crumbly. Make a well in dry ingredients; add milk, stirring until mixture just comes together.

Bake fruit mixture for 10 minutes. Remove from oven. Using a 3-tablespoon scoop, drop dough over fruit. Sprinkle with coarse sugar. Bake until biscuits are golden brown and fruit is bubbly, 35 to 40 minutes.

miniature peach cobblers

Go ahead and dog-ear this page. While the ripe Southern peaches are divine, what keeps me coming back is the buttery almond biscuit topping. The recipe makes extra topping, which you can freeze and keep on hand for when cobbler cravings strike. **SERVES 6**

ALMOND BISCUIT TOPPING

- 1¼ cups all-purpose flour
- ½ cup sugar
- 1½ teaspoons baking powder
- 1 teaspoon kosher salt
- 6 tablespoons cold unsalted butter, cubed
- ½ cup heavy whipping cream
- ½ cup sliced almonds

FILLING

- 6 cups peeled, pitted, and sliced fresh peaches
- 2 tablespoons unsalted butter
- 2 tablespoons fresh orange juice
- 1 tablespoon fresh lemon juice
- 1 cup sugar
- 2 teaspoons cornstarch
- ½ teaspoon ground cinnamon
- ¼ teaspoon ground nutmeg

ALMOND BISCUIT TOPPING In a large bowl, whisk together flour, sugar, baking powder, and salt. Using 2 forks or a pastry blender, cut butter into flour mixture until crumbly. Make a well in dry ingredients; add cream and almonds, stirring until mixture just comes together. (Mixture will be crumbly.)

Using your hands, gently shape dough into a disk; divide in half. Wrap in plastic wrap, and refrigerate until ready to use.

FILLING Preheat oven to 350°. In a large saucepan, combine peaches, butter, orange juice, and lemon juice, and cook over medium heat, stirring occasionally, until butter is melted, about 8 minutes. In a medium bowl, whisk together sugar, cornstarch, cinnamon, and nutmeg; stir into peach mixture until combined. Remove from heat.

Divide peach mixture among 6 (1½-cup) ovenproof dishes. Divide one portion of Almond Biscuit Topping into 6 pieces; place over peach mixture. Place on a rimmed baking sheet. Bake until browned and bubbly, 25 to 28 minutes.

fresh cherry-almond cobbler

Fresh cherries are such a treat, and I love how jammy they get when cooked down in this cobbler. Serve this with a generous scoop of vanilla ice cream and an extra sprinkle of toasted almonds.

SERVES 6 TO 8

2½ **pounds pitted fresh cherries (about 5 cups)**
1 **cup granulated sugar, divided**
1 **cup all-purpose flour, divided**
2 **tablespoons fresh lemon juice**
¼ **teaspoon almond extract**
½ **cup almond flour**
1 **teaspoon kosher salt**
¾ **teaspoon baking powder**
6 **tablespoons cold unsalted butter, cubed**
½ **cup whole buttermilk**
Garnish: sliced almonds, confectioners' sugar

Preheat oven to 350°.

In a large bowl, stir together cherries, ¾ cup granulated sugar, ¼ cup flour, lemon juice, and almond extract. Spoon cherry mixture into a 2-quart baking dish.

In a medium bowl, whisk together almond flour, salt, baking powder, remaining ¼ cup granulated sugar, and remaining ¾ cup flour. Using 2 forks or a pastry blender, cut butter into flour mixture until crumbly. Make a well in dry ingredients; add buttermilk, stirring until mixture just comes together. (Dough will be wet.) Drop dough over cherry mixture.

Bake until browned and bubbly, 40 to 50 minutes. Let cool for 10 minutes. Garnish with almonds and confectioners' sugar, if desired.

individual nectarine & raspberry cobblers

Dessert's just a little more fun when you get your very own personal dish that you don't have to share! Feel free to mix up the fruit—switch out the nectarines for plums or peaches, if you like. **MAKES 8**

2/3 cup plus 4 tablespoons sugar, divided
1/4 cup cornstarch
1 1/2 teaspoons lemon zest
4 cups peeled, pitted, and sliced fresh nectarines (about 8 nectarines)
3 (6-ounce) containers fresh raspberries
1 1/2 cups all-purpose flour
1 1/2 teaspoons baking powder
1/2 teaspoon kosher salt
1 1/2 cups heavy whipping cream

Preheat oven to 400°.

In a small bowl, combine 2/3 cup sugar, cornstarch, and zest.

In a large bowl, toss together nectarines, raspberries, and sugar mixture until fruit is evenly coated. Divide fruit among 8 (6- to 8-ounce) ramekins.

In a medium bowl, whisk together flour, 2 tablespoons sugar, baking powder, and salt. Pour cream into flour mixture, and stir with a wooden spoon just until combined. Divide dough among ramekins, placing on top of fruit mixture. Sprinkle dough with remaining 2 tablespoons sugar.

Bake until biscuits are golden brown and fruit is bubbly, about 25 minutes. Let cool slightly before serving.

homestyle peach cobbler

There are two camps when it comes to cobbler—those who crave more fruit, and those who demand more topping. Topping lovers, this one is for you. The extra fat from the whipping cream allows the topping to spread, baking into a sweet blanket of biscuit goodness. **SERVES 8**

5   cups sliced peeled fresh peaches or 2 (20-ounce) packages frozen sliced peaches, thawed
1½   cups granulated sugar, divided
1½   cups all-purpose flour, divided
1   teaspoon almond extract
1½   teaspoons baking powder
¾   teaspoon kosher salt
6   tablespoons cold unsalted butter, cubed
½   cup heavy whipping cream
1   tablespoon white sparkling sugar

Preheat oven to 350°.

In a 2½-quart baking dish, place peaches. Sprinkle with 1 cup granulated sugar, ¼ cup flour, and almond extract; stir to combine.

In a medium bowl, whisk together baking powder, salt, remaining ½ cup granulated sugar, and remaining 1¼ cups flour. Using 2 forks or a pastry blender, cut butter into flour mixture until crumbly. Make a well in dry ingredients; add cream, stirring until mixture just comes together.

Tear dough into 3-inch round pieces; arrange over peach mixture. Sprinkle with sparkling sugar.

Bake until browned and bubbly, 35 to 40 minutes. Let cool for 10 minutes before serving.

blackberry cobbler

When it comes to cooking, sometimes it's OK to cheat a little bit. Frozen biscuits can be a huge timesaver, and while they're not quite as perfect as homemade, they'll do in a pinch. **SERVES 12**

9   **cups fresh blackberries**
1   **cup plus 1 tablespoon sugar, divided**
6   **tablespoons all-purpose flour**
1   **(24-ounce) package frozen bite-size buttermilk tea biscuits***
1   **tablespoon unsalted butter, melted**
¼   **teaspoon ground cinnamon**

We used Mary B's.

Preheat oven to 350°.

In a large bowl, combine blackberries, 1 cup sugar, and flour. Spoon into a 13x9-inch baking dish. Bake for 20 minutes. Remove from oven.

Place biscuits on a baking sheet. Bake for 10 minutes. Remove biscuits from baking sheet, and place on blackberry mixture. Brush biscuits with melted butter.

In a small bowl, combine cinnamon and remaining 1 tablespoon sugar. Sprinkle over biscuits.

Bake until browned and bubbly, about 20 minutes.

lemon-poppyseed shortcakes

Essentially biscuits' sweeter sisters, shortcakes lend themselves to a multitude of dessert imaginings. These lemon-poppyseed ladies are also spectacular with ripe strawberries. **MAKES 12**

½ cup apricot jam
3 cups fresh blueberries
2 cups all-purpose flour
½ cup plus 2 tablespoons granulated sugar, divided
2 tablespoons lemon zest
2 teaspoons poppy seeds
2 teaspoons baking powder
¼ teaspoon baking soda
½ cup cold unsalted butter, cubed
1¼ cups heavy whipping cream, divided
½ cup whole buttermilk
1 teaspoon vanilla extract
1 large egg white, lightly beaten
¼ cup confectioners' sugar
Garnish: lemon slices

Preheat oven to 400°. Line a baking sheet with parchment paper. In a small saucepan, heat apricot jam over medium heat. Add blueberries, tossing gently to coat; remove from heat. Set aside.

In a medium bowl, whisk together flour, ½ cup granulated sugar, zest, poppy seeds, baking powder, and baking soda. Using 2 forks or a pastry blender, cut butter into flour mixture until crumbly.

In another medium bowl, whisk together ¼ cup cream, buttermilk, and vanilla. Make a well in dry ingredients; add cream mixture, stirring until mixture just comes together. (Dough will be sticky.)

On a lightly floured surface, roll dough 1 inch thick. Using a 2½-inch round cutter dipped in flour, cut 12 circles, rerolling scraps as needed. Place on prepared pan. Brush with egg white, and sprinkle with remaining 2 tablespoons granulated sugar. Bake until lightly browned, 12 to 14 minutes. Let cool completely on a wire rack.

In a medium bowl, beat confectioners' sugar and remaining 1 cup cream with a mixer at medium speed until stiff peaks form. Cut shortcakes in half horizontally. Layer blueberries and whipped cream on bottom halves; cover with top halves. Garnish with lemon slices, if desired.

strawberry cobbler

This skillet version of strawberry shortcake is a simple, yet show-stopping dessert. Be sure to use an enamel-coated cast-iron skillet to ensure the strawberry filling is ruby red and delicious. **SERVES 6 TO 8**

6   cups quartered fresh strawberries (about 2 pounds)
1   cup sugar
¼   cup cornstarch
1   large egg, lightly beaten
1   teaspoon lime zest
1   tablespoon fresh lime juice
½   teaspoon ground cinnamon
¼   teaspoon kosher salt

BISCUIT TOPPING
2   cups self-rising flour
⅓   cup plain cornmeal
⅓   cup granulated sugar
½   cup cold unsalted butter, cubed
⅔   cup whole buttermilk
1   tablespoon coarse sugar

Vanilla ice cream, to serve

Preheat oven to 350°. Spray a 10-inch enamel-coated cast-iron skillet with cooking spray.

In a large bowl, stir together strawberries, sugar, cornstarch, egg, lime zest and juice, cinnamon, and salt. Transfer to prepared skillet.

BISCUIT TOPPING In a medium bowl, whisk together flour, cornmeal, and granulated sugar. Using 2 forks or a pastry blender, cut butter into flour mixture until crumbly. Make a well in dry ingredients; add buttermilk, stirring until mixture just comes together. Drop 3-inch pieces of dough over strawberry mixture. Sprinkle with coarse sugar.

Bake until browned and bubbly, 45 to 50 minutes, loosely covering with foil to prevent excess browning, if necessary. Serve with ice cream.

rosemary shortcakes with apple-plum sauce

These aren't your grandmother's shortcakes. This twist on the classic is fun to serve guests—the flavor combination is unexpected, and they're easy to make ahead of time. **MAKES 4**

2   cups self-rising flour
2½   tablespoons sugar
1   teaspoon finely
        chopped fresh rosemary
¼   teaspoon kosher salt
½   cup unsalted butter,
        softened
¼   cup whole milk
2   tablespoons heavy
        whipping cream

APPLE-PLUM SAUCE
1   cup water
⅔   cup sugar
¼   cup red wine vinegar
3   plums, peeled and
        sliced
1   Granny Smith apple,
        peeled and sliced
1   teaspoon orange zest

WHIPPED CREAM
1   cup heavy whipping
        cream
½   cup confectioners'
        sugar

Preheat oven to 400°. Line a baking sheet with parchment paper. In a large bowl, whisk together flour, sugar, rosemary, and salt. Using 2 forks or a pastry blender, cut butter into flour mixture until crumbly. Make a well in dry ingredients; gradually add milk, stirring until mixture just comes together. Divide dough into 4 equal portions, and pat into 3-inch circles on prepared pan. (See note.) Brush dough with cream. Bake until golden brown, about 10 minutes. Let cool, and cut in half horizontally.

SAUCE In a large saucepan, bring 1 cup water, sugar, and vinegar to a boil. Cook until syrupy, about 10 minutes. Add plums, apples, and zest; cook until fruit is tender, about 8 minutes.

WHIPPED CREAM In a large bowl, beat cream with a mixer at medium-high speed until soft peaks form. Gradually add confectioners' sugar, beating until stiff peaks form.

Spoon fruit and sauce over bottom half of shortcakes. Top with whipped cream, and cover with top halves.

NOTE: When forming shortcakes, make sure to pack the dough together so they won't crumble during cutting.

peaches & cream shortcakes

Simmered with vanilla and spices, peaches make an excellent filling for these sweet and crunchy brown sugar shortcakes. **MAKES 6**

1½   **cups all-purpose flour**
¼   **cup firmly packed light brown sugar**
2   **teaspoons baking powder**
¼   **teaspoon kosher salt**
4½   **tablespoons cold unsalted butter, cubed**
½   **cup plus 2 tablespoons heavy whipping cream, divided**
½   **teaspoon vanilla extract**
1   **tablespoon granulated sugar**

PEACH FILLING
2   **(16-ounce) bags frozen peaches**
½   **cup firmly packed brown sugar**
¼   **cup heavy whipping cream**
½   **teaspoon ground cinnamon**
½   **teaspoon vanilla extract**

Sweetened whipped cream

Garnish: toasted coconut

Preheat oven to 350°. Line a baking sheet with parchment paper.

In a large bowl, whisk together flour, brown sugar, baking powder, and salt. Using 2 forks or a pastry blender, cut butter into flour mixture until crumbly. Make a well in dry ingredients; add ½ cup cream and vanilla, stirring until mixture just comes together.

Turn out dough onto a lightly floured surface, and roll ½ inch thick. Using a 3-inch round cutter dipped in flour, cut 6 biscuits, rerolling scraps once. Place biscuits 2 inches apart on prepared pan. Brush tops with remaining 2 tablespoons cream, and sprinkle with granulated sugar. Bake until lightly browned, about 20 minutes.

PEACH FILLING In a large saucepan, combine peaches, brown sugar, whipping cream, cinnamon, and vanilla. Cook over medium-low heat until peaches are tender, about 10 minutes.

Cut Brown-Sugar Shortcakes in half horizontally, and place bottom halves on 6 dessert plates. Spoon peach mixture over each half. Cover with top halves and whipped cream. Garnish with coconut, if desired.

SIMPLE
Quick
Breads

WHEN YOU'RE CRAVING
SOMETHING SWEET AND EASY,
NOTHING'S BETTER THAN THESE
COMFORTING QUICK BREADS

easy lemon bread

Because quick breads are so easy, it's tempting to throw everything but the kitchen sink into the bowl. This recipe is divinely simple, accented with the sweet tartness of fresh lemon. **SERVES 6**

½ cup unsalted butter, softened
1¼ cups sugar, divided
2 large eggs
1¼ cups all-purpose flour
1 teaspoon double-acting baking powder
¼ teaspoon kosher salt
½ cup whole milk
1 teaspoon lemon zest
¼ cup fresh lemon juice

Preheat oven to 350°. Spray a 9x5-inch loaf pan with baking spray with flour.

In a large bowl, beat butter and 1 cup sugar with a mixer at medium speed until fluffy, 3 to 4 minutes, stopping to scrape sides of bowl. Add eggs, one at time, beating well after each addition.

In a medium bowl, sift together flour, baking powder, and salt. Gradually add flour mixture to butter mixture alternately with milk, beginning and ending with flour mixture, beating just until combined after each addition. Stir in zest. Pour batter into prepared pan.

Bake until a wooden pick inserted in center comes out clean, about 1 hour. Place pan on a wire rack. Using a wooden skewer, poke holes in bread.

In a small bowl, combine lemon juice and remaining ¼ cup sugar. Pour mixture over hot bread. Let cool completely in pan.

honey monkey bread

My friend Emily came up with this recipe when we were on a quest to change up the traditional butter-sugar-cinnamon monkey bread routine. Doused in golden honey, this ooey-gooey recipe is a sweet and sticky delight! **SERVES 10**

½ **cup sugar**
4 **(7.5-ounce cans) refrigerated buttermilk biscuits**
1¼ **cups honey**
½ **cup unsalted butter**
½ **teaspoon ground cinnamon**

Preheat oven to 350°. Spray a 15-cup tube pan with cooking spray.

In a large resealable plastic bag, place sugar. Separate biscuits, and cut into quarters. Place biscuits in sugar, shaking to coat. Layer biscuits in prepared pan.

In a small saucepan, heat honey, butter, and cinnamon over medium-high heat until butter is melted. Pour over biscuits.

Bake for 30 minutes, loosely covering with foil to prevent excess browning, if necessary. Let cool in pan for 10 minutes. Invert pan onto a serving plate. Serve immediately.

classic banana bread

Thank goodness for Southern ports like New Orleans and Charleston—their early imports of tropical goodies made ingredients like bananas indispensable in our favorite Southern recipes. Try toasting a slice of this comforting quick bread in a buttered skillet for a breakfast treat. **MAKES 1 (9-INCH) LOAF**

⅓ cup whole buttermilk
1 teaspoon baking soda
½ cup unsalted butter, softened
1 cup sugar
2 large eggs
2¼ cups all-purpose flour
½ teaspoon kosher salt
½ teaspoon ground cinnamon
¼ teaspoon ground nutmeg
1½ cups mashed banana (about 3 medium bananas)
1 teaspoon vanilla extract

Preheat oven to 325°. Spray bottom only of a 9-inch loaf pan with baking spray with flour.

In a small bowl, stir together buttermilk and baking soda; let stand for 5 minutes.

In a large bowl, beat butter and sugar with a mixer at medium speed until fluffy, 3 to 4 minutes, stopping to scrape sides of bowl. Add eggs, one at a time, beating well after each addition.

In a medium bowl, whisk together flour, salt, cinnamon, and nutmeg. With mixer on low speed, gradually add flour mixture, buttermilk mixture, and banana to butter mixture. Beat in vanilla. Spoon batter into prepared pan, smoothing top with an offset spatula.

Bake until a wooden pick inserted in center comes out clean, about 1 hour and 10 minutes. Let cool in pan for 10 minutes. Remove from pan, and let cool completely on a wire rack.

orange-cardamom loaves

I can still remember my first sniff of cardamom, from an ancient tin buried in the back of my mother's spice cabinet. Its complex aroma is so deliciously unique, and pairs nicely with the floral citrus flavor of orange in this quick bread. **MAKES 2 (8X4-INCH) LOAVES**

3   cups all-purpose flour
1½ teaspoons kosher salt
1½ teaspoons baking
      powder
2½ cups sugar
1½ cups whole milk
1   cup vegetable oil
3   large eggs
2   tablespoons orange
      zest
1½ teaspoons vanilla
      extract
¼   teaspoon ground
      cardamom
Orange Glaze (recipe
      follows)

ORANGE GLAZE
2   cups confectioners'
      sugar
1   teaspoon orange zest
⅓   cup fresh orange juice

Preheat oven to 350°. Spray 2 (8x4-inch) loaf pans with baking spray with flour.

In a medium bowl, sift together flour, salt, and baking powder.

In a large bowl, beat sugar, milk, oil, eggs, zest, vanilla, and cardamom with a mixer at medium speed until combined. Gradually add flour mixture to sugar mixture, beating until smooth. Divide batter between prepared pans.

Bake for 30 minutes. Loosely cover with foil, and bake until a wooden pick inserted in center comes out clean, about 30 minutes more.

Let cool in pans for 10 minutes. Remove from pans, and let cool completely on a wire rack.

GLAZE In a medium bowl, whisk together confectioners' sugar and orange zest and juice until smooth. Drizzle glaze over cooled loaves.

apple-pecan monkey bread

With chunks of tart Granny Smith apple drenched in a buttery, cinnamon-laced caramel sauce, this monkey bread has all the flavors of apple pie, but it's so much simpler to prepare. **SERVES 10 TO 12**

½   **cup granulated sugar**
2   **teaspoons pumpkin pie spice**
2   **(16.3-ounce) cans refrigerated buttermilk biscuits**
1   **apple, peeled, cored, and cubed**
½   **cup chopped pecans**
½   **cup unsalted butter**
⅓   **cup firmly packed light brown sugar**
½   **cup apple butter**

Preheat oven to 350°. Spray a 15-cup Bundt pan with baking spray with flour.

In a large bowl, stir together granulated sugar and pumpkin pie spice. Cut biscuits into quarters; toss in sugar mixture to coat. Layer coated biscuits, apple, and pecans in prepared pan.

In a small saucepan, heat butter and brown sugar over medium-high heat, stirring until sugar is dissolved, about 4 minutes. Remove from heat; stir in apple butter. Pour sugar mixture over layered biscuits, apple, and pecans in pan.

Bake until golden brown, about 35 minutes. Let cool in pan for 10 minutes. Invert onto a serving platter. Serve warm.

poppyseed-pecan bread

Who knows how Southerners came to love poppy seeds so much, but I'm willing to venture a theory as to why—it's the crunch they add to cakes, muffins, and quick breads. This recipe from my friends at the Georgia Pecan Commission doubles down on this theory with the added buttery crunch of pecans. **MAKES 2 (9X5-INCH) LOAVES**

3   large eggs
2½ cups sugar
1½ cups whole milk
1   cup plus 2 tablespoons
     vegetable oil
2   tablespoons poppy
     seeds
1   teaspoon vanilla
     extract
1   cup chopped pecans
3   cups all-purpose flour
1½ teaspoons kosher salt
1½ teaspoons baking
     powder

GLAZE
¾   cup sugar
¼   cup fresh orange juice

Preheat oven to 350°. Spray 2 (9x5-inch) loaf pans with baking spray with flour.

In a large bowl, beat eggs, sugar, milk, and oil with a mixer at medium speed until combined. Stir in poppy seeds and vanilla; fold in pecans.

In a medium bowl, stir together flour, salt, and baking powder. Stir flour mixture into egg mixture until smooth. Divide batter between prepared pans.

Bake until a wooden pick inserted in center comes out clean, about 55 minutes. Remove from pans, and let cool completely on a wire rack.

GLAZE In a small saucepan, combine sugar and orange juice over medium heat. Bring to a boil; cook for 5 minutes, stirring constantly. Spoon glaze over bread. Let glaze cool completely before slicing.

hummingbird quickbread

One of the many things that quick breads have going for them is that, since they are technically bread and not cake, you can make the case that they're perfectly acceptable for breakfast. **MAKES 1 (9-INCH) LOAF**

2   cups all-purpose flour
1   cup sugar
½   cup sweetened flaked
       coconut, toasted
½   cup toasted pecans, chopped
1½   teaspoons baking powder
1   teaspoon ground cinnamon
½   teaspoon baking soda
½   teaspoon kosher salt
¼   teaspoon ground nutmeg
¼   teaspoon ground allspice
¼   teaspoon ground ginger
1   (8-ounce) can crushed
       pineapple, drained
1   cup mashed ripe banana
¾   cup canola oil
2   large eggs
1   teaspoon vanilla extract
Cream Cheese Glaze (recipe follows)
Garnish: ground cinnamon

CREAM CHEESE GLAZE
⅔   cup confectioners' sugar
¼   cup cream cheese, softened
¼   teaspoon vanilla extract
1   tablespoon whole milk
1 to 2 tablespoons fresh
       lemon juice

Preheat oven to 350°. Spray a 9-inch loaf pan with baking spray with flour.

In a large bowl, combine flour, sugar, coconut, pecans, baking powder, cinnamon, baking soda, salt, nutmeg, allspice, and ginger. Make a well in center of dry ingredients. In a medium bowl, combine pineapple, banana, oil, eggs, and vanilla. Add pineapple mixture to flour mixture, stirring just until moistened. Spoon into prepared pan.

Bake until a wooden pick inserted in center comes out clean, about 55 minutes. Let cool in pan for 10 minutes. Run a knife around edges of loaf; remove from pan, and let cool completely on a wire rack.

Drizzle with Cream Cheese Glaze. Garnish with cinnamon, if desired.

CREAM CHEESE GLAZE In a small bowl, whisk together confectioners' sugar, cream cheese, vanilla, milk, and enough lemon juice until glaze reaches desired consistency.

sweet potato bread with candied pecans

I start dreaming about sweet potato bread in July, when it's way too hot to even say the word "oven" aloud. But I can't help it—it's a kind of therapy for me; a promise that fall will indeed come after all. When temperatures do drop, this recipe will be waiting. **MAKES 1 (9-INCH) LOAF**

2   cups all-purpose flour
1½ teaspoons ground cinnamon
½   teaspoon baking powder
½   teaspoon baking soda
½   teaspoon kosher salt
¼   teaspoon ground allspice
1¼ cups firmly packed light
      brown sugar
½   cup unsalted butter, melted
1   (15-ounce) can cut sweet
      potatoes in syrup,* drained
      and coarsely mashed
2   large eggs
1   teaspoon vanilla extract
½   teaspoon lemon zest
Cream Cheese Glaze (recipe on
      page 112)
Candied Pecans (recipe follows)

We used Bruce's.

CANDIED PECANS
1   large egg white
¼   cup sugar
1   teaspoon water
⅛   teaspoon kosher salt
⅛   teaspoon ground cinnamon
1½ cups pecan halves

Preheat oven to 350°. Spray a 9-inch loaf pan with baking spray with flour. In a large bowl, whisk together flour, cinnamon, baking powder, baking soda, salt, and allspice; make a well in center of flour mixture. In a medium bowl, whisk together brown sugar, melted butter, sweet potatoes, eggs, and vanilla. Pour over flour mixture, and beat with a mixer at low speed until combined. Stir in zest. Spoon batter into prepared pan, smoothing top.

Bake until a wooden pick inserted in center comes out clean, about 50 minutes. Let cool in pan for 10 minutes. Remove from pan, and let cool completely on a wire rack. Drizzle Cream Cheese Glaze over bread. Sprinkle with Candied Pecans.

CANDIED PECANS Preheat oven to 250°. Line a rimmed baking sheet with foil, and spray with cooking spray.

In a medium bowl, whisk together egg white, sugar, 1 teaspoon water, salt, and cinnamon until foamy. Add pecans; toss well. Using a slotted spoon, place pecans on prepared pan. Spread in an even layer. Bake until dry to the touch, about 1 hour, stirring occasionally. Let cool completely.

skillet monkey bread

I'm a firm believer that just about everything's better in a skillet. This monkey bread makes a great easy dessert for any breakfast or brunch gathering. The toasted coconut on top adds a nice sweet crunch. **SERVES 6**

1	(16.3-ounce) can refrigerated buttermilk biscuits
½	cup unsalted butter, melted
¾	cup sugar
2	teaspoons ground cinnamon
⅓	cup chopped pecans
⅓	cup sweetened flaked coconut
	Cane syrup or maple syrup, to serve

Preheat oven to 350°. Spray a 10-inch oven-safe skillet with cooking spray.

Cut biscuits into quarters. In a small bowl, place melted butter. In another small bowl, stir together sugar and cinnamon. Working in batches, dip biscuit pieces in melted butter; roll in sugar mixture to coat. Place biscuit pieces in prepared pan. Sprinkle with pecans and coconut.

Bake until golden brown, about 25 minutes. Let cool for 15 minutes. Drizzle with cane syrup or maple syrup, if desired.

zucchini bread with buttermilk-lemon glaze

The bountiful blessing (and curse!) of Southern gardens, zucchini sneaks its way into many an old Southern recipe, because we just can't bring ourselves to waste it. This bread is a great way to use up your bumper crop. **MAKES 1 (8X5-INCH) LOAF**

2   cups all-purpose flour
¾   cup granulated sugar
½   cup toasted pecans, chopped
2   teaspoons baking powder
½   teaspoon baking soda
½   teaspoon ground nutmeg
½   teaspoon kosher salt
1   cup shredded zucchini (about 1 medium zucchini)
⅔   cup whole milk
⅓   cup unsalted butter, melted
2   teaspoons lemon zest
1   large egg
⅓   cup confectioners' sugar, sifted
2   teaspoons whole buttermilk
1   teaspoon fresh lemon juice

Preheat oven to 350°. Spray an 8x5-inch loaf pan with baking spray with flour.

In a large bowl, stir together flour, granulated sugar, pecans, baking powder, baking soda, nutmeg, and salt. Add zucchini, stirring to combine. In a small bowl, stir together milk, melted butter, zest, and egg. Pour over flour mixture, stirring just until moistened. Spoon batter into prepared pan.

Bake until a wooden pick inserted in center comes out clean, about 50 minutes. Let cool in pan for 10 minutes. Remove from pan, and let cool completely on a wire rack.

In a small bowl, stir together confectioners' sugar, buttermilk, and lemon juice until smooth. Drizzle over bread.

quick monkey bread rolls

My friend Christy Jordan is the queen of quick and easy Southern cooking, and these sweet bites are one of her many delicious creations. She came up with these single-serving treats to surprise her children, but I haven't met an adult who's passed one up. **MAKES 10**

1   (12-ounce) can refrigerated buttermilk biscuits
6   tablespoons unsalted butter, melted
½   cup granulated sugar
½   cup firmly packed light brown sugar
1   teaspoon ground cinnamon
½   cup maple syrup

Preheat oven to 350°. Spray 10 muffin cups with baking spray with flour.

Cut biscuits into thirds. Pour melted butter into a medium bowl. In another medium bowl, stir together sugars and cinnamon. Dip biscuit pieces into butter; dredge in sugar mixture. Place 3 biscuit pieces in each prepared muffin cup.

Bake until puffed and golden brown, 12 to 15 minutes. Let stand for 5 minutes. Run a knife around edge of cups to remove rolls. Drizzle with maple syrup.

BISCUIT
Toppings

SPOONED OVER OR SLATHERED INSIDE,
THESE GRAVIES AND SPREADS TAKE
YOUR FAVORITE BISCUITS OVER THE TOP

blackberry jam

One taste of this easy homemade jam, and you'll forsake storebought versions forever. Dolloped over a pat of melting butter, it's a divine topper for your favorite biscuits. **MAKES 7 PINTS**

8 **cups fresh blackberries**
6 **cups sugar**
1 **Granny Smith apple, peeled, cored, and grated**
Juice of 1 lemon

In a large enamel-coated Dutch oven, combine berries, sugar, and apple. Using a potato masher, mash berry mixture.

Bring to a boil over medium-high heat, stirring frequently. Reduce heat to medium.

Cook, stirring frequently, until mixture comes to a rolling boil, 40 to 50 minutes. Add lemon juice during the last 10 minutes of cooking.

Remove from heat and transfer to clean, sterilized jars. Refrigerate for up to two weeks.

chocolate gravy

I'd never heard of chocolate gravy until I started working at Taste of the South *magazine. I don't know how I lived so long without it.*

MAKES 3 CUPS

¼   cup salted butter
½   cup sugar
⅓   cup natural unsweetened cocoa powder
2   tablespoons all-purpose flour
2½   cups whole milk
1   teaspoon vanilla extract

In a medium saucepan, melt butter over medium heat. Add sugar, cocoa, and flour, stirring to combine.

Add milk and vanilla; whisk until no lumps remain. Simmer until thickened, about 4 minutes. Serve hot with biscuits.

sawmill gravy *(photo on page 128)*

When you need a breakfast that'll keep you going all day, nothing beats a biscuit topped with this hearty sausage gravy.   **MAKES 4 CUPS**

1   (1-pound) package ground pork sausage
¼   cup all-purpose flour
4   cups whole milk
1   teaspoon garlic salt
½   teaspoon ground black pepper
½   teaspoon Worcestershire sauce

In a large skillet, cook sausage over medium-high heat, stirring occasionally, until browned and crumbly, about 12 minutes.

Sprinkle flour over sausage, and stir until sausage is coated. Gradually whisk in milk; simmer, whisking constantly, until thickened, about 4 minutes. Stir in garlic salt, pepper, and Worcestershire.

tomato gravy

Rich with the flavors of smoky bacon and tomatoes, this gravy makes a great topper for brunch biscuits. **MAKES 4 CUPS**

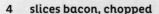

4 slices bacon, chopped
½ cup chopped white onion
3 tablespoons all-purpose flour
1 (14.5-ounce) can diced tomatoes
2 cups tomato juice
1 cup chicken broth
½ teaspoon kosher salt
¼ teaspoon ground black pepper

In a large skillet, cook bacon and onion over medium-high heat until bacon is crisp and onion is softened, about 6 minutes.

Stir in flour; cook for 1 minute. Add tomatoes, tomato juice, and broth; bring to a simmer. Stir in salt and pepper.

SAWMILL GRAVY
(page 127)

CHOCOLATE GRAVY
(page 127)

red-eye gravy

Born in leaner times, this classic Southern gravy is about as simple as it gets. Be sure to use country ham; the extra salt makes all the difference. **MAKES 4 CUPS**

4   (¼-inch-thick) slices country ham

⅔   cup strong-brewed coffee

In a large skillet, cook ham in batches over medium heat until browned, about 6 minutes. Remove from skillet, reserving drippings in skillet.

Increase heat to medium-high. When drippings begin to smoke, add coffee, scraping browned bits from bottom of pan. Simmer for 2 minutes, stirring occasionally. Serve with biscuits and ham, if desired.

TOMATO GRAVY

RED-EYE GRAVY

SWEET & SPICY
HONEY

ORANGE
& GINGER
HONEY

sweet & spicy honey

Also known as bee sting honey, this pepper-spiked condiment takes a fried chicken biscuit over the top. **MAKES 1 CUP**

1	cup honey
1	tablespoon crushed red pepper
1	tablespoon apple cider vinegar

In a small saucepan, heat all ingredients over medium heat. Cook until honey begins to bubble around edges of pan. Remove from heat, and let cool. Refrigerate for up to 2 weeks

orange & ginger honey

Infused with citrus and spice, this honey is especially delicious drizzled over warm sweet potato biscuits. **MAKES 1 CUP**

1	cup honey
6	(2-inch) strips orange zest, divided
2	ounces fresh ginger slices
2	tablespoons unsalted butter

In a small saucepan, bring honey, 5 orange zest strips, and ginger to a boil over medium heat. Remove from heat; stir in butter. Let stand for 30 minutes.

Remove and discard orange zest and ginger. Place remaining orange zest in a glass jar. Pour infused honey into jar. Cover and refrigerate for up to 2 weeks.

spiced pear butter

Slow cookers are one of the most divine kitchen tools; they make short work of recipes like this sweet pear butter. If you prefer, substitute apples for equally delicious results. **MAKES 4 CUPS**

12	Bartlett pears, peeled and chopped (about 2½ pounds)
2	cups firmly packed light brown sugar
½	cup apple cider vinegar
½	cup cane syrup
2	tablespoons ground cinnamon
2	tablespoons fresh lemon juice
1	tablespoon ground cardamom
1	tablespoon vanilla extract
2	teaspoons ground allspice
1	teaspoon kosher salt
½	teaspoon ground cloves
¼	teaspoon ground nutmeg

In a 5-quart slow cooker, stir together all ingredients.

Cover and cook on high for 6 to 8 hours, stirring every hour. Using a potato masher, finely mash pears.

Cover and cook on low for 6 hours.

In the container of a blender, purée pear mixture until smooth. Transfer to airtight containers. Refrigerate for up to 2 weeks.

INDEX

A

Almond Biscuit Topping **81**

Angel Biscuits **30**

Apple-Plum Sauce **94**

Apple-Pecan Monkey Bread **108**

B

Bacon-Cheddar Biscuits **34**

Blackberry Cobbler **89**

Blackberry Jam **124**

Black Pepper & Thyme Biscuits **56**

Black Pepper & Parmesan Biscuits with Roast Beef **41**

Brisket & Biscuits **50**

Buttermilk Biscuits with Sausage Gravy **25**

C

Candied Pecans **115**

Cat Head Biscuits **29**

Chicken & Dumplings Skillet Casserole **59**

Chicken Biscuits **38**

Cheese-Pepper Biscuits **53**

Chocolate Chip Biscuits **22**

Chocolate Gravy **127**

Classic Banana Bread **104**

Classic Beef Brisket **50**

Cornmeal Drop Biscuits **64**

D

Dill & Cornmeal Drop Biscuits **72**

Drop Biscuits **26**

E

Easy Lemon Bread **100**

F

Fresh Cherry-Almond Cobbler **82**

G

Glazed Ham **45**

H

Homestyle Peach Cobbler **86**

Honey Monkey Bread **103**

Hummingbird Quickbread **112**

I

Individual Nectarine & Raspberry Cobblers **85**

L

Lemon-Poppyseed Shortcakes **90**

M

Miniature Peach Cobblers **81**

O

Orange & Ginger
  Honey **131**
Orange-Cardamom
  Loaves **107**
Orange Glaze **107**

P

Peaches & Cream
  Shortcakes **97**
Pecan Goat Cheese
  Biscuits **75**
Pecan Pimiento Cheese **46**
Pimiento Cheese & Bacon
  Biscuit Sandwiches **46**
Poppyseed-Pecan
  Bread **111**

Q

Quick Monkey Bread
  Rolls **120**

R

Red-Eye Gravy **129**
Rolled Biscuits **26**
Rosemary Shortcakes with
  Apple-Plum Sauce **94**

S

Sausage Gravy **25**
Savory Cobbler with
  Sausage & White Beans **71**
Sawmill Gravy **127**
Skillet Monkey Bread **116**
Snickerdoodle Biscuits **18**
Spiced Pear Butter **132**
Spicy Cheddar Biscuits
  with Glazed Ham **45**
Strawberry Cobbler **93**
Sunday Chicken & Biscuit
  Pot Pie **63**
Sweet & Spicy Honey **131**
Sweet Potato Biscuits **21**

Sweet Potato Bread with
  Candied Pecans **115**
Sweet Potato Drop
  Biscuits **67**

T

Toad in a Biscuit **29**
Tomato Cobbler **49**
Tomato Gravy **128**
Triple Berry Cobbler **78**
Turkey Pot Pie **68**

W

Whipped Cream **94**
White Cheddar Biscuits
  with Fresh Herbs **60**
Whole Wheat Biscuits **33**

Z

Zucchini Bread with
  Buttermilk-Lemon
  Glaze **119**